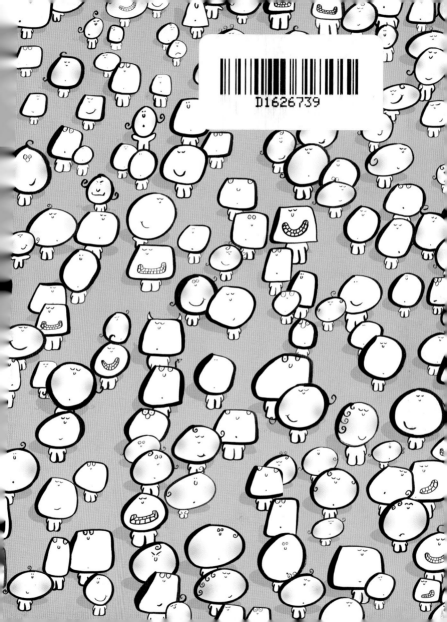

chocolate

with Vimrod

chocolate

life is a struggle between good, evil and chocolate

Vimrd by Lisa Swerling and Ralph Lazar

HarperCollins*Publishers*

See no chocolate,
hear no chocolate,
speak no chocolate.

(get hospitalised due to
chocolate deprivation.)

if you inherited
a million dollars,
would you invest
it or spend it on
chocolate?

my new year's
resolution
is to start
thinking
about beginning
to **consider**
eating less
chocolate

i am guilty of procrastination.

i can't decide whether to eat all this chocolate **now** or in five minutes' time.

i slay
dragons
for
chocolate

i spy with my little eye
something beginning

with **choc**
and ending with

lit

i only eat
free-range
chocolates

my favourite colour is
chocolate

actually, forget the
mushrooms and anchovies.
if i could just have a

sprinkling of chocolate

on my pizza, that
would be great.

scientists

have created genetically modified sheep that poo chocolate.

i am going to get my shepherd's licence.

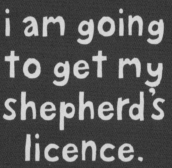

if there were only **two** chocolate bars left on planet earth and they took refuge in your home, would you:

1. hand them over to the **government**?

2. let them **breed**?

3. **eat** them?

my doctor recommended

chocolate

therapy

i don't love chocolate

i love chocolate<u>s</u>

i am **happy**
because today
i am going to eat
one point three
kilograms of
chocolate

danger. easily aggravated.
subdue immediately with
chocolate.

have you
ever
met a box of
chocolates
you didn't
like?

are two of the UK's most familiar
graphic artists. Through their company
Last Lemon they have spawned a catwalk
of popular cartoon characters, which
includes Harold's Planet, The Brainwaves,
Blessthischick and, of course, Vimrod.

Writers, artists and designers, they are
married with two children, and spend
their time between London and various
beaches on the Indian Ocean.

- -

HarperCollins*Publishers*

77–85 Fulham Palace Road, Hammersmith, London W6 8JB

www.harpercollins.co.uk

Published by HarperCollins*Publishers* 2007

1

A catalogue record for this book is available from the British Library

ISBN-10   0 00 724206 9

ISBN-13   978 0 00 724206 1

Set in Bokka

Printed and bound in Italy by Lego SpA

other titles in the **Vimrod** collection:

drink!
Wine is made to be drunk,
I am drunk,
therefore
am I wine?

Vimrod by Lisa Swerling & Ralph Lazar

shopping
it's the little voices that tell me to
go shopping

Vimrod by Lisa Swerling and Ralph L...

farting
my farts hospitalise small children

Vimrod by Lisa Swerling & Ralph Lazar

xmas
christmas is **coming run!**

Vimrod ...RLING & RALPH LAZAR

love
You and me...
...two hamsters on the spinning-wheel of **life**

Vimrod by Lisa Swerling and Ralph Lazar

dads
life is a journey between the **fridge** and the **sofa**

Vimrod by Lisa Swerling and Ralph Lazar

mums
behind every **great woman** is her **bum**

Vimrod by Lisa Swerling and Ral...

(watch this space)

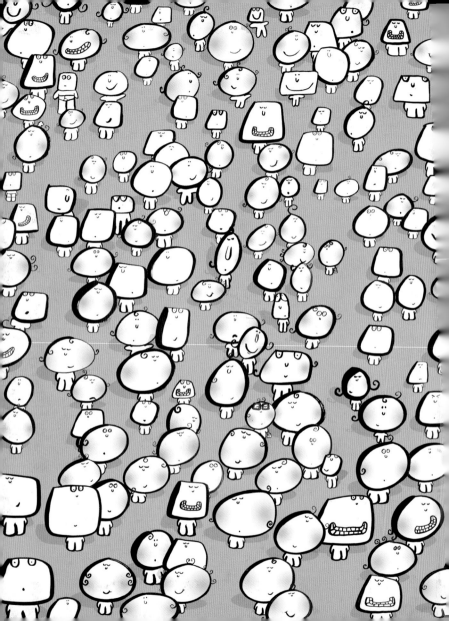